Other giftbooks by Helen Exley

...And Wisdom Comes Quietly
A Special Gift of Peace and Calm
My Wishes For You
Words on Kindness
Thank You for Every Little Thing

Published simultaneously in 2002 by Exley Publications Ltd
in Great Britain, and Exley Publications LLC in the USA.

4 6 8 10 12 11 9 7 5 3

ISBN 1-86187-429-4

Edited by Helen Exley.
Illustrated by Juliette Clarke.
Printed in China.

Exley Publications Ltd
16 Chalk Hill, Watford, Herts WD19 4BG, UK

Exley Publications LLC,
185 Main Street, Spencer, MA 01562, USA

www.helenexleygiftbooks.com

A SPECIAL GIFT

THANK YOU FOR YOUR KINDNESS

Illustrated by Juliette Clarke

A HELEN EXLEY GIFTBOOK

FAMILIAR ACTS
ARE BEAUTIFUL
THROUGH LOVE.

PERCY BYSSHE SHELLEY (1792-1822)

HOW BEAUTIFUL
A DAY CAN BE WHEN
KINDNESS TOUCHES IT.

ELLISSON

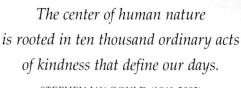

*The center of human nature
is rooted in ten thousand ordinary acts
of kindness that define our days.*

STEPHEN JAY GOULD (1941-2002)

*One kind word can warm
three winter months.*

JAPANESE PROVERB

*Kindness is gladdening the hearts
of those who are travelling in the dark
with us....*

HENRI FRÉDERIC AMIEL (1821-1881)

*Kindness spreads so quickly,
you couldn't stop it even if you tried!*

SIAN E. MORGAN, B.1973

THE POWER OF KINDNESS

*Kindness seems a feeble thing
set against the heroic acts
of which humanity is capable.
Yet it eases us all through life.*

PETER GRAY, B.1928

*When you give and receive kindness
you are automatically richer
than a millionaire.*

NATASHA CLARKSON, B.1973

*Patience and courtesy and kindness
can transform a life.*

PAM BROWN, B.1928

KINDNESS SNOWBALLS...
AND ALONG ITS PATH
IT FLATTENS ANGER, JEALOUSY,
SADNESS AND DESPAIR.

SIAN E. MORGAN, B.1973

A kind heart is a fountain
of gladness, making everything
in its vicinity freshen into smiles.

WASHINGTON IRVING
(1783-1859)

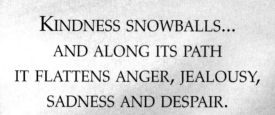

Here's to all the little things,
the "done-and-then-forgotten" things,
Those "oh-it's-simply-nothing" things
That make life worth the fight.

AUTHOR UNKNOWN

Small kindnesses, small courtesies,
small acts of friendship,
can transform the day.
Just a chat, a cup of tea, a lift to the shops,
the collection of a prescription,
the caring for a cat,
a listening and a patient ear,
a pot of jam, a bunch of flowers,
the first beans of the year.
A smile. A wave.
A scrap of cheerful gossip.

PAM BROWN, B.1928

To remember names, to remember

likes and dislikes, to remember anniversaries

– that is the beginning of kindness.

PAMELA DUGDALE

YOU LIFTED ME...

You turned an awful day
into a great one,
you lifted me out of the blues,
you restored my faith
in human nature
and you made all
the difference.

SIAN E. MORGAN, B.1973

Thank you for simply
being you
– constant in friendship,
unfailing in kindness.

JANE SWAN, B.1943

*Through you I learned how great life can be,
how the simple things in life are really the most
important and how you treat other people
is really all that matters.*

LISA SCULLY-O'GRADY

*Thank you for making me feel life is worth
having, whatever happens.*

PAM BROWN, B.1928

Thank you that you <u>are</u>,
Thank you for just being!

HELEN THOMSON, B.1943

*Joy spreads like ripples on a pond.
Thank you for chucking those large pebbles.*

JAMES GIBSON, B.1953

A WORLD OF KINDNESS

The birds in my garden

kindly serenade me awake.

The milkman kindly leaves milk

for my morning coffee.

The local schoolboy

kindly delivers my newspaper.

I haven't even left the house yet

and already my day is full of kindness.

SIAN E. MORGAN, B.1973

Kindness holds the world together.

PAM BROWN, B.1928

*A hundred times a day I remind myself
that my inner and outer life depends
on the labours of other men, living and dead,
and that I must exert myself to give
in the same measure as I have received.*

ALBERT EINSTEIN (1879-1955)

*THANK YOU TO THE PEOPLE
WHO OPENED MY EYES,
MY EARS, MY MIND, MY HEART.*

PAM BROWN, B.1928

*I awoke this morning with devout
thanksgiving for all my friends.*

RALPH WALDO EMERSON
(1803-1882)

...A TRUE FRIEND

*It is not so much our friends' help
that helps us as the confident knowledge
that they will help us.*

EPICURUS (341-270 B.C.)

*Friendship, a dear balm...
A smile among dark frowns:
a beloved light:
A solitude, a refuge, a delight.*

PERCY BYSSHE SHELLEY (1792-1822)

The one thing
I know my friends have in common
is that they are all kind.
And that's the only thing
I'll ever need to know.

SIAN E. MORGAN, B.1973

WHOEVER KNOWS
HOW TO RETURN A KINDNESS
IS A FRIEND
ABOVE ALL PRICE.

SOPHOCLES
(496-406 B.C.)

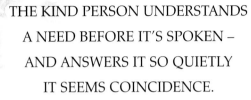

THE KIND PERSON UNDERSTANDS
A NEED BEFORE IT'S SPOKEN –
AND ANSWERS IT SO QUIETLY
IT SEEMS COINCIDENCE.

PAMELA DUGDALE

*Sometimes the greatest kindness
is simply to listen.*

PAM BROWN, B.1928

*The kindness I have longest remembered
has been of this sort, the sort unsaid;
so far behind the speaker's lips
that almost it already lay in my heart.
It did not have far to go to be
communicated.*

HENRY DAVID THOREAU (1817-1862)

One of the most beautiful qualities
is to understand and to be understood.

SENECA (4 B.C. – 65 A.D.)

Often... you cannot completely alleviate
someone's problem but by being with them,
by being for them, whatever you can do
for them makes a difference.

BROTHER GEOFF, GENERAL SERVANT OF
THE MISSIONARIES OF CHARITY BROTHERS

No act of courage,
kindness, understanding
is ever lost.
It is a pebble thrown
into a lake.
Its ripples spread out
to the very end
of time.

PAM BROWN, B.1928

THE BIG EFFECT OF KINDNESS

The kindness and love of one single person
can change the lives of thousands.

CHARLOTTE GRAY, B.1937

How far that little candle throws his beams!
So shines a good deed in a naughty world.

WILLIAM SHAKESPEARE (1564-1616)

Each time someone stands up for an ideal or
acts to improve the lot of others or strikes out
against injustice, he sends forth a tiny ripple
of hope, and crossing each other from a million
different centers of energy and daring, those
ripples build a current that can sweep down
the mightiest walls of oppression and resistance.

ROBERT KENNEDY (1925-1968)

"I ADMIRE KIND PEOPLE"

Kindness has taken a bad rap in many ways,
being associated with weakness or meekness
or labels like "goody-goody."
But true kindness comes from strength,
and is full of life....

BO LOZOFF

THE HIGHEST WISDOM IS KINDNESS.

THE GEMARA (C.500), FROM "THE TALMUD"

When I was young, I admired clever people.
Now that I am old, I admire kind people.

ABRAHAM HESCHEL (1907-1972)

Kindness is the first of all virtues.

MARQUIS DE VAUVENARGUES (1715-1747)

LIFE IS MOSTLY FROTH AND BUBBLE,
TWO THINGS STAND LIKE STONE,
KINDNESS IN ANOTHER'S TROUBLE,
COURAGE IN YOUR OWN.

ADAM LINDSAY GORDON (1833-1870)

AT A SAD TIME...
THANK YOU FOR YOUR KINDNESS

FRIENDS STAND THERE AS A SOLID
AND IMPREGNABLE BULWARK AGAINST
ALL THE EVILS OF LIFE.

SYDNEY SMITH (1771-1845)

NO ONE IS USELESS IN THIS WORLD
WHO LIGHTENS THE BURDEN
OF IT FOR ANYONE ELSE.

CHARLES DICKENS (1812-1870)

I never crossed your threshold with a grief,
but that I went without it.

THEODOSIA GARRISON (1874-1944)

Thank you for all the times when I thought
I didn't need you, but you were there anyway
to give me a helping hand when things went
terribly wrong.

LISA SCULLY-O'GRADY

"Thank you" seems such a clichéd, repeated,
automated worn-out old thing to say.
And what you've done for me doesn't deserve
two hackneyed, tired words. Just know that
you've given me so much help and happiness,
that you have buttressed my life.

HELEN THOMSON, B.1943

WHEN HOPE FAILS

There is no need to go searching for a remedy

for the evils of the time.

The remedy already exists – it is the gift

of one's self to those who have fallen

so low that even hope fails them.

RENÉ BAZIN (1853-1932)

*No one is as capable of gratitude as one
who has emerged from the kingdom of night.*

ELIE WIESEL, B.1928

*A FRIEND IS THE ONE
WHO COMES IN WHEN THE WHOLE
WORLD HAS GONE OUT.*

ALBAN GOODIER

YOU

*Your friendship has been
the sunlight that has
transformed my days.*

PAM BROWN, B.1928

*You believe in me.
There are no trite words of thanks that
could tell you what that means to me.*

INGEBORG NELSON

*I watch you help, when you are laden with bags.
I watch you share your lunch,
even though you are hungry.
I watch as you listen carefully,
even though you are rushed.
And I hope that some day
Your kindness will be returned to you.*

SIAN E. MORGAN, B.1973

VERY SPECIAL GIFTS

*Giving presents is a talent; to know what a
person wants, to know when and how to get it,
to give it lovingly and well.*

PAMELA GLENCONNER (1871-1928)

*Other people's gifts are useful,
sensible or totally expected. Yours come
in strange-shaped packages and wheeze
or click or rattle – or lie still, but still
defy all guessing. Things like
six-footed cuddly crocodiles.
Exotic shells. Chinese groceries.
An abacus. A flapping seagull. Toys.
With you, I can always say,
with all my heart,
"Oh! I've always wanted one of those!"*

PAM BROWN, B.1928

WHAT IS THE BEST GIFT
YOU EVER RECEIVED?
BETTER STILL, WHAT IS THE BEST
GIFT YOU EVER GAVE?
PERHAPS YOU WILL RECALL
THAT IN EACH INSTANCE,
THE BEST GIFT WAS ONE...
THAT INCLUDED A PART OF SELF.

WANDA FULTON

QUIET TIME, THE TOUCH
OF A HAND, A SMILE

TO BE KIND CAN BE A SMILE, A WORD,

THE OPENING OF A DOOR, AN OFFER

OF ASSISTANCE — OR IT CAN BE,

MORE USEFULLY, THE SCRUBBING OF

A FLOOR, THE COOKING OF A MEAL,

A WASHING LOAD, A CAR-BOOT FULL

OF SHOPPING, A LIFT TO THE HOSPITAL

IN THE EARLY HOURS,

A NEVER-ENDING PATIENCE.

PAM BROWN, B.1928

True kindness is not flowers and violins
but time and patience
and the strength of steel.

PETER GRAY, B.1928

MEDICINES MAY BE NECESSARY.
FLOWERS LIFT THE HEART.
BUT YOUR SMILE IS THE BEST
RESTORATIVE OF ALL.

PAM BROWN, B.1928

Some days the best
of kindness is a simple note,
a short call.

MARGOT THOMSON, B.1943

COMFORT...

Kindness wraps us round like a warm,
comforting shawl – a gentleness,
a thoughtfulness, a concern for our well-being
that lifts the saddest heart.

PETER GRAY, B.1928

–

I THOUGHT I WAS ALONE;
THEN SOMEONE
SENT ME FLOWERS.

CHRISTINA ANELLO

–

OTHER PEOPLE ARE SYMPATHETIC,

CONCERNED, KIND

– BUT NEVER THERE.

YOU ARE – WHENEVER I MOST NEED YOU.

PAM BROWN, B.1928

–

"THANK YOU" WILL NEVER BE ENOUGH

I can no other answer make but thanks
And thanks, and ever thanks.

WILLIAM SHAKESPEARE (1564-1616)

Some people give unconditionally. Mothers do,
grandmothers do and husbands for wives.
Lifelong friends do. They give a lifetime. You do.
And "thank you" will never be enough.

HELEN EXLEY

Surely there's something more impressive
in the dictionary than a lame "thank you"!
It doesn't begin to express what I feel about you,
the support you've been to me.

MARGOT THOMSON, B.1943

Thank You
I could shout the words from the highest
mountain for all the world to hear.
I could paint the words across the moon
for all the world to see.
I could cast the words in bronze
for all the world to feel.
But, however I proclaim my thanks,
there is no way to fully show
you how grateful I am.

STUART MACFARLANE, B.1953

YOU HAVE STOOD BESIDE ME

I CAN NEVER THANK YOU ENOUGH
BECAUSE YOU HAVE BEEN THERE,
YOU HAVE STOOD BESIDE ME,
YOU HAVE PROPPED ME UP,
AND LET ME DOWN GENTLY.
YOU HAVE REBUILT ME
AND MADE ME STRONG.
I AM A TOWER
OF YOUR THOUGHTS AND CARE.
THANK YOU.

GREETINGS CARD INSCRIPTION,
AUTHOR UNKNOWN

*Thank you for being with us
through it all –
for the warm pressure of your love
and the immediacy of your grace.*

DOUGLAS GIFFORD

*Thank you for phoning me
on evenings full of winter gloom.
Just to say hello.*

PAM BROWN, B.1928

YOU WERE ALWAYS THERE.
NO ONE ELSE WAS.

HELEN EXLEY

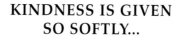

KINDNESS IS GIVEN
SO SOFTLY...

Kindness is given so softly, so gently,
falling like tiny seeds along our paths –
and brightening them with flowers.

PAM BROWN, B.1928

If someone listens,
or stretches out a hand, or whispers
a kind word of encouragement,
or attempts to understand a lonely person,
extraordinary things begin to happen.

LORETTA GIRZARTIS, B.1920

A look of sympathy, of encouragement;

a hand reached out in kindness.

All else is secondary.

MAYA V. PATEL, B.1943

It may not be a resounding obituary –

an accolade in the nobler

Sunday newspapers

– but "she was kind"

celebrates a life that was not wasted.

CHARLOTTE GRAY, B.1937

Kind words can be short and easy

to speak, but their echoes are endless.

MOTHER TERESA (1910-1997)

What do we live for,
if it is not to make life less difficult
for each other?

GEORGE ELIOT (MARY ANN EVANS) (1819-1880)

–

Only a life lived for others is worth living.

ALBERT EINSTEIN (1879-1955)

–

WHEN A PERSON DOES A GOOD DEED
WHEN HE OR SHE DIDN'T HAVE TO,
GOD LOOKS DOWN AND SMILES
AND SAYS,
"FOR THIS MOMENT ALONE,
IT WAS WORTH CREATING THE WORLD."

THE TALMUD

–

KINDNESS REMEMBERED

*Kindnesses are like summer flowers
slipped between the pages of a book –
their messages of affection springing to
life again in a few years.*

PAM BROWN, B.1928

KINDNESS IS NEVER FORGOTTEN.

PETER GRAY, B.1928

Gratitude is the memory of the heart.

J.B. MASSIEU (1742-1822)

*Looking back, we remember the clever,
the ingenious, the spectacular
– but most of all,
we remember the kind.*

PAMELA DUGDALE

What is a *Helen Exley Giftbook*?

Helen Exley has been creating giftbooks for twenty-six years, and her readers have bought forty-eight million copies of her works, in over thirty languages. Because her books are all bought as gifts, she spares no expense in making sure that each book is as thoughtful and meaningful a gift as it is possible to create: good to give, good to receive. Kindness and friendship are very strong in Helen's books and she has now created several titles on these themes.

Team members help to find thoughtful quotations from literally hundreds of sources, and the books are then personally created. With infinite care, Helen ensures that each illustration matches each quotation, that each spread is individually designed to enhance the feeling of the words, and that the whole book has real depth and meaning.

You have the result in your hands. If you have loved it – tell others! We'd rather put the money into more good books than waste it on advertising when there is no power on earth like the word-of-mouth recommendation of friends.

Helen Exley Giftbooks
16 Chalk Hill, Watford, Herts WD19 4BG, UK
185 Main Street, Spencer, MA 01562, USA
www.helenexleygiftbooks.com

Acknowledgements: The publishers are grateful for permission to reproduce copyright material. Whilst every reasonable effort has been made to trace copyright holders, we would be pleased to hear from any not here acknowledged. PAM BROWN, NATASHA CLARKSON, PAMELA DUGDALE, HELEN EXLEY, JAMES GIBSON, CHARLOTTE GRAY, PETER GRAY, STUART MACFARLANE, SIAN E. MORGAN, INGEBORG NELSON, MAYA V. PATEL, LISA SCULLY-O'GRADY, JANE SWAN, HELEN THOMSON, MARGOT THOMSON: published with permission © Helen Exley 2002.